$19.50
3.99

Time: 1947

Cornerstones of Freedom

Chuck Yeager Breaks the Sound Barrier

R. Conrad Stein

CHILDREN'S PRESS®
A Division of Grolier Publishing
New York • London • Hong Kong • Sydney
Danbury, Connecticut

Library of Congress Cataloging-in-Publication Data

Stein, R. Conrad.
Chuck Yeager breaks the sound barrier / R. Conrad Stein.
    p. cm.— (Cornerstones of freedom)
    Includes index.
    Summary: Relates how the young pilot distinguished himself in
World War II and subsequently became the first person to break the
sonic barrier.
    ISBN 0-516-20294-4 (lib.bdg.)   0-516-26137-1 (pbk.)
    1. Yeager, Chuck, 1923—-Juvenile literature. 2. Air pilots—United
States—Biography—Juvenile literature. 3. High-speed aeronautics—
History—Juvenile literature.   [1. Yeager, Chuck,1923–. 2. Air pilots.
3. High-speed aeronautics—History.] I. Title. II. Series.
TL540.Y4S74 1997
629.13`092—dc20
                                                    [B] 96-26203
                                                          CIP
                                                          AC

When the United States entered World War II in 1941, German aircraft swarmed in the skies above Europe. German pilots were hailed as the best in the world. Because the United States desperately needed its own pilots, the U.S. Air Force allowed young men—some only in their teens—to enter flight school. One of those trainees was nineteen-year-old Chuck Yeager. From the beginning, Yeager amazed his flight-school instructors. His talent for flying was a natural gift, one that could not be taught.

Chuck Yeager was only nineteen years old when he began flight training in the U.S. Air Force.

P-51 Mustang fighter planes, similar to the one that Chuck Yeager was flying when he was shot down over France

In early 1944, at age twenty-one, Yeager was sent to England to fly combat missions. He would be flying a plane called the P-51 Mustang, a propeller-driven plane frequently used in combat. It was equipped with machine guns on each wing that could be controlled by the pilot. Yeager was eager to sharpen his skills by flying against tough German aviators. On Yeager's ninth mission, a German aircraft slipped behind the young American. The German pilot blasted Yeager's Mustang with machine gun fire. "The world exploded," Yeager later wrote in his autobiography. "I ducked to protect my face with my hands, and when I looked up a second later, my engine was on fire." Fighting to open his airplane's canopy, Yeager squeezed out of the cockpit. He parachuted to the ground in a wooded area somewhere in German-occupied France.

Scrambling to his feet, Yeager realized that his leg was covered with blood. Although badly wounded, he didn't feel much pain. In the distance, he heard army trucks and voices shouting in German. He found a hiding place in some bushes and waited until dark. Through the sleepless night, Yeager watched and waited. Early the next morning, he spotted a French woodsman and approached him. The woodsman did not speak English, and Yeager did not speak French. Yeager pointed to his uniform and attempted to explain that he was an American pilot who needed help.

Finally, the Frenchman led Yeager to a unit of the French Underground. The French Underground was a secret organization of men and women, mostly farmers and workers, who fought the German army occupying their country. One of its tasks was to rescue British and American fliers whose planes were shot down over France. Members of the Underground took Yeager to a secluded farmhouse where he received food and medical treatment.

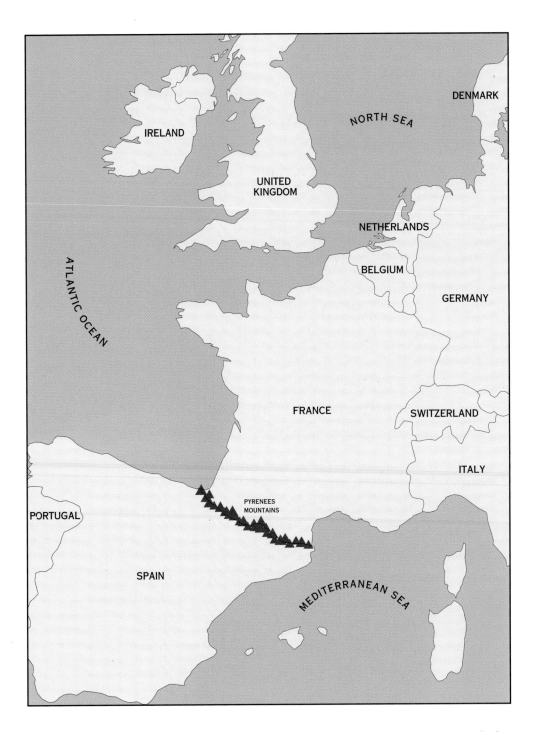

In 1944, Germany occupied many European countries, including France. With the help of the French Underground, Chuck Yeager escaped across the Pyrenees Mountains from German-occupied France to Spain.

With the help of the French Underground, Yeager began a twenty-five-day journey that led him to the Spanish border. Spain was a neutral country, which means it was not involved in the war. During his trek, Yeager helped the members of the Underground set fuses for bombs. The bombs were used to blow up German munitions trains and to destroy bridges that were key to the German war effort. It was very dangerous work. Enemy patrols hunted for French Underground members constantly. When captured, they were tortured and executed.

During the course of Yeager's journey to the Spanish border, several other American pilots who had recently been shot down over France joined his group. Finally, the exhausted pilots and their guides reached the snow-covered Pyrenees Mountains, which mark France's border with Spain. Members of the Underground pointed out the proper direction to go, but the Americans had to cross the mountains on their own. A short distance from the safety of the Spanish border, Yeager and a bomber pilot were spotted by a German squad. The Germans opened fire. A bullet struck the bomber pilot in the knee. Yeager helped the wounded man and both slid down a snowy mountain ridge. Incredibly, they escaped from the Germans and crossed the border to Spain, where Yeager contacted American authorities.

Back at a base in England, Yeager convinced his superior officers to return him to combat. His quickness during aerial combat and aggressive flying tactics earned him a reputation as one of the United States's best aviators. Yeager was able to spot enemy planes flying 50 miles (80 kilometers) away, where they appeared as tiny specks among the clouds. Yeager once shot down five German planes in one mission—the highest single-day total ever achieved by an American.

Yeager impressed his superior officers with his natural abilities as an aviator.

During World War II, propeller-driven planes were used in aerial combat. A propeller-driven craft uses curved blades connected at their centers to provide power for movement. Planes, helicopters, and boats are propeller-driven craft. In 1944, however, Germany introduced the first jet fighter, called the Messerschmitt Me 262. A jet fighter is much more powerful than a propeller-driven plane because its fuel is discharged in bursts, called jets, that give the plane the ability to fly very fast. The Messerschmitt Me 262 had two jet engines and could fly at speeds of 550 miles (885 km) per hour.

The German-made Messerschmitt Me 262, with a top speed of 550 miles (885 kilometers) per hour, was the first jet aircraft.

In a propeller-driven craft, the P-51 Mustang, Chuck Yeager shot down a German jet fighter.

While flying on patrol during the fall of 1944, Yeager spotted a Messerschmitt Me 262. Yeager was once again flying the P-51 Mustang. The Mustang's top speed was 450 miles (724 km) per hour. That was 100 mph (161 kph) slower than the German jet that Yeager had spotted. Yeager attempted to sneak up behind the German plane, but it quickly zoomed to safety. In his slower aircraft, Yeager felt like he was riding a bicycle and trying to catch up to a speeding car. Minutes later, though, Yeager noticed another Me 262 that was slowly approaching a landing field. Yeager quickly opened fire. He later wrote, "My hits slapped into his wings. . . . I looked back and saw the jet crash-landing short of the runway, sheering off a wing in a cloud of dust and smoke." Yeager had accomplished what seemed to be impossible—he had shot down a jet while piloting a propeller-driven airplane.

Despite his victory, Chuck Yeager knew that jets and rocket-propelled airplanes were the future of aviation. He hoped that one day he would have a chance to fly one.

After World War II ended in 1945, Yeager decided to stay in the U.S. Air Force. As one of the nation's most talented pilots, he was given the job of testing new aircraft, including the United States's earliest jets. When he first took off in a jet fighter called the Lockheed P-80 Shooting Star, he felt a great surge of power pinning him back in his seat. In the new jet, Yeager was able to reach a speed of 550 miles (885 km) per hour, an unmatched speed for American pilots of his era.

The Lockheed P-80 Shooting Star was one of the first jet fighters developed by the United States.

Orville Wright (on plane) and his brother, Wilbur (right) were responsible for the world's first flight, which took place in Kitty Hawk, North Carolina, on December 17, 1903.

In May 1947, Chuck Yeager volunteered to test-fly an experimental rocket plane called the Bell X-1. More than just an aircraft, it was a laboratory with wings. The Bell X-1 was designed to fly faster than the speed of sound— a feat never before accomplished by an airplane carrying a human being.

In 1947, the sound barrier loomed as the greatest challenge to aviators. At sea level, sound travels at 761 miles (1,225 km) per hour. High in the sky, above 45,000 feet (13,716 meters), the speed of sound is about 660 miles (1,062 km) per hour. In the 44-year history of flight, which began in 1903 with the Wright brothers' first flight, no pilot had ever been able to travel faster than the speed of sound. In a power dive, which occurs when a plane accelerates while making a sharp descent, propeller-driven planes had come close to reaching the speed of sound. But strange things happened to aircraft as they neared the sound barrier. The planes bounced violently like cars traveling over bumpy roads. Pilots reported that their controls stopped working, making it difficult to pull out of the power dive.

On September 27, 1946, a British test pilot named Geoffrey de Havilland Jr. attempted to break the sound barrier in a new type of jet aircraft. De Havilland, who was the son of a famous airplane manufacturer, was killed. His plane apparently shook itself to pieces as it approached the speed of sound. After that, many aircraft designers believed aviators would never be able to break the sound barrier.

Geoffrey de Havilland Jr.

Engineers believed that replacing the wide, blunt nose of propeller-driven fighters (below) with a sharp, pointed nose would allow a plane (the Bell X-1, right) to cut through the sound barrier like a bullet.

But other designers claimed the speed of sound was not really a barrier. They explained that the shaking that occurred as a plane neared the speed of sound was caused by a condition called "compressibility." As an aircraft drew close to the speed of sound, the air in front of it could not move aside fast enough, so it became bunched up (compressed). The compressed air formed an invisible wall that pressed against the front of the aircraft. But, claimed the designers, this wall of compressed air could be penetrated by a specially constructed plane with a powerful engine. Bolder engineers had already pointed out that bullets broke the sound barrier every time they were fired from a gun. The designers suggested that constructing a plane similar to the way a bullet is constructed—narrower toward the front and wider toward the back— would enable a plane to pierce the wall of compressed air. Yeager, a self-taught aircraft engineer, agreed with the designers.

The Bell X-1 airplane that Yeager volunteered to test had a pointed nose, with thin, sharp-edged wings that could cut through the compressed air like a knife. The small plane measured only 31 feet (9 meters) long with a 28-foot (45-m) wingspan. Four rocket motors made the Bell X-1 a very powerful aircraft. Yeager named the plane *Glamorous Glennis,* after his wife, Glennis Yeager. He hoped that his wife's name on the plane's nose would bring him good luck.

Chuck Yeager climbs into the cockpit of Glamorous Glennis.

Flight tests on the Bell X-1 took place over Muroc Airfield Base in southern California. Today, Muroc Airfield Base is called Edwards Air Force Base, and it remains a testing ground for advanced planes and spacecraft. During the day, temperatures can rise to 120° F (49° C). At night, the outside air often drops below freezing. In 1947, authorities liked Muroc because of the

The dry lake bed at Muroc Airfield Base (now called Edwards Air Force Base) is the perfect location for a landing strip.

privacy of its location in the desert. But most important, the base featured a dry lake bed that measured 7 miles (11 km) long and 5 miles (8 km) wide. With its surface baked hard by the sun, the lake bed made a perfect landing strip for high-speed airplanes.

Scientists call the speed of sound "Mach 1," after a famous Austrian scientist named Ernst Mach. Nine test flights on the Bell X-1 were scheduled to gradually increase the plane's speed to Mach 1 in degrees of tenths. A flight that was planned to go seven-tenths the speed of sound was described as .7 Mach; eight-tenths was .8 Mach. The counting continued upward until Mach 1 (the speed of sound) was finally attained.

Engineers were concerned that the Bell X-1 could not hold enough fuel to take off under its own power and still achieve high speeds. So the tiny plane was lashed to the underbelly of a giant B-29 bomber, which carried it into the air. For safety reasons, Yeager sat as a passenger inside the B-29 bomber during takeoff. At about 10,000 feet (3,048 m), he began the tricky maneuver of climbing down into the tiny cockpit of the *Glamorous Glennis*. Once Yeager settled into the cockpit, the B-29 climbed to an altitude of about 25,000 feet (7,620 m). From there, Yeager and the Bell X-1 were dropped like a rock off a building.

Falling away from the bomber from such a height was very dangerous. If anything went wrong, Yeager could not bail out of *Glamorous Glennis.* The plane had a side-opening door, which meant he would be cut in half by the plane's wing if he tried to jump out. Despite the dangers, Yeager savored the thrill of the flight. With rockets roaring, the plane shot forward like an arrow.

On his sixth flight, Yeager reached .86 Mach. There he felt the terrible wall of compressed air in front of his craft. The plane lurched and began to spin out of control. His right wing dropped, but he could do nothing to correct it.

Summoning all his skills as a pilot, he managed to slow the plane down and land safely.

On the seventh flight, Yeager pushed the plane up to .94 Mach, where he endured an even scarier experience. After the plane began shaking, he eased back on the controls, attempting to take the plane higher. But nothing happened. He was soaring through the sky with no control over his plane. Yeager was able to slow the aircraft by releasing some of its fuel. Once again, he landed safely.

If Yeager had tried to abandon his mission by jumping out of Glamorous Glennis, *the plane's wing (behind Yeager) could have sliced his body in half.*

The difficulties Yeager and the team of flight engineers encountered in trying to break the sound barrier did not discourage them. The attempt to reach Mach 1 was scheduled for the ninth test flight, on October 14, 1947.

The day before the flight, Yeager took his wife, Glennis, to dinner at a roadside restaurant called the Fly Inn, which was owned by a woman named Pancho Barnes. During the 1920s and 1930s, Pancho had secretly flown rifles to revolutionaries in Mexico who were

Pancho Barnes was one of the first female aviators.

attempting to overthrow the Mexican government. Pancho was a very good friend of Chuck Yeager. After Chuck and Glennis finished dinner, Pancho loaned them two of her horses and suggested they take an evening ride in the desert. An hour later, as they galloped back to the corral, Chuck did not notice that the corral gate had been closed. The horse he was riding stopped short, and Yeager somersaulted over the animal's head. When he hit the ground, he broke two of his ribs.

Chuck (center) and Glennis Yeager

But Chuck was determined to break the sound barrier during the next test flight. He refused to let his injury keep him from the attempt. Glennis drove him into town, where a civilian doctor taped up his ribs. Yeager did not want an Air Force doctor to know about the accident because he didn't want to be disqualified from flying. Despite the tape, Yeager felt unbearable pain when he used his right arm with any force. Yet he needed to use that arm to lock the cockpit door of the Bell X-1. Finally he told a friend, Jack Ridley, about his predicament. Ridley was an engineer on the Bell X-1 team. Ridley sawed off a 10-inch (25-centimeter) piece of broomstick and attached it to the door handle of the plane. The stick would be a lever so that Yeager could reach over and lock the door with his left hand.

High in the sky the next day, October 14, Yeager climbed down the ladder from the B-29 into the Bell X-1. He felt the pain of his cracked ribs, but with the aid of Ridley's ingenious broomstick handle, he managed to lock the airplane's door. Once settled, he radioed to the bomber pilot that he was clear to drop.

The Bell X-1 fell free from the bomber. Yeager dipped toward earth, picking up speed. Next he leveled out and flipped a switch to fire his rockets. At .88 Mach the plane began to shake violently, but Yeager continued on. At 42,000 feet (12,802 m) the flight became smooth. Yeager felt as if he were still on the ground. Yeager glanced at his Mach needle and it suddenly began to fluctuate. Yeager later wrote; "It went up to .96 Mach — then flipped right off the scale. I thought I was seeing things!" Chuck Yeager had finally broken the sound barrier.

Jack Ridley devised a way for the injured Chuck Yeager to close the plane door.

Chuck Yeager emerges from the Glamorous Glennis *following his historic flight.*

For almost twenty seconds, Yeager streaked through the sky at this previously unheard-of rate of speed. He marveled at the plane's power as he realized he was still accelerating. On the ground, the crew was shaken by a thunderous bang that sounded like an explosion. But in the airplane all was silent. Instruments later showed that the plane had reached Mach 1.07, about 700 miles (1,127 km) per hour.

His fuel exhausted, Yeager glided back toward the desert landing strip. When he spotted the ground crew, Yeager put the *Glamorous Glennis* into a series of victory rolls.

On the ground, the Bell X-1 team members shook hands and slapped each other on the back. Everyone knew they had made history. But they were the only ones who knew. The tests on the plane had been conducted under a shroud of military secrecy, so the breakthrough remained a secret. No newspaper headlines announced Yeager's triumph, even though it was the most significant aviation accomplishment since the Wright brothers first took to the air in 1903. In spite of the secrecy, Chuck, Glennis, and the Bell X-1 team members celebrated the historic flight with a steak dinner at the Fly Inn.

It was not until June 1948, eight months after the flight, that the U.S. Air Force announced that the sound barrier had

President Harry Truman (left) congratulates Chuck Yeager on his supersonic accomplishment at a White House ceremony on December 17, 1948.

been broken. By that time, Yeager had flown the Bell X-1 faster than the speed of sound more than a dozen times in subsequent test flights. The thunderous bang, heard during the historic October flight, had become a routine sound at Muroc Airfield Base. It became known as the sonic boom. When the great feat of supersonic flight was finally revealed to the public, President Harry Truman invited Chuck Yeager to the White House. At last the public could acknowledge the tremendous breakthrough achieved by Yeager and his team of engineers.

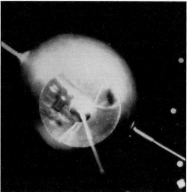

Above: The Soviet satellite Sputnik I *was the first artificial satellite to orbit the Earth. Right: Yuri Gagarin, a Soviet cosmonaut (astronaut) and the first human being to orbit the Earth.*

The first American to orbit the Earth was John Glenn Jr.

In 1947, Chuck Yeager accomplished a feat that many aviators thought was impossible. Since then, aviation has made great advances and improvements. In fact, some people believe that the first step in the space age was taken when Chuck Yeager broke the sound barrier.

Space travel officially began on October 4, 1957, when the Soviet Union launched **Sputnik I,** *the first artificial satellite to orbit the Earth. The first manned space flight occurred on April 12, 1961, when a Soviet cosmonaut (astronaut) named Yuri Gagarin orbited the Earth in a spaceship. In May 1961, American astronaut Alan Shepard Jr. made a 15-minute space flight, but he did not go into orbit. The first American to orbit the Earth was John Glenn Jr., on February 20, 1962.*

During the years that followed, technology for space flight improved so quickly that the first human beings reached the moon on July 20, 1969, on the Apollo XI spacecraft. U.S. astronauts Neil Armstrong and Edwin "Buzz" Aldrin Jr. walked on the moon and conducted experiments for nearly twenty-two hours before returning to orbit.

Above: The Apollo 11 *lunar module, called* Eagle, *which carried astronauts Neil Armstrong and Edwin "Buzz" Aldrin Jr. to the moon. The Earth is in the background.*

Left: Astronaut Neil Armstrong took this photograph of Buzz Aldrin. They were the first human beings to walk on the moon.

Chuck Yeager remained in the U.S. Air Force and became famous as the country's best test pilot. Over the years, he flew more-advanced jet and rocket aircraft. He often reached speeds exceeding two and three times the speed of sound. By the time he retired from the Air Force in 1975, Yeager had been promoted to the rank of brigadier general.

In the summer of 1950, *Glamorous Glennis* was delivered to the Smithsonian Institution in Washington, D.C. It now hangs from the ceiling of the Smithsonian's National Air and Space Museum. The little orange plane is a prized

member of a display called "Milestones of Flight." *Glamorous Glennis* hangs between the Wright brothers' original aircraft and the *Apollo XI* space capsule. Without Chuck Yeager and *Glamorous Glennis,* the incredible human accomplishment of space travel would not have been possible.

The National Air and Space Museum in Washington, D.C.

GLOSSARY

accelerate – to move faster or gain speed

aviation – anything related to the operation, manufacture, development, and design of aircraft

bomber – airplane designed to drop bombs on specific targets

canopy – the roof, or top, of an airplane's cockpit

civilian – person who does not serve in the military

cockpit – place in an airplane where the pilot sits

propeller-driven

munitions – ammunition; materials necessary for combat

nose – the front end of a plane

propeller-driven – anything that uses blades to provide power for movement; planes, helicopters, and boats are propeller-driven

shroud – to cover with secrecy

streamline

sonic boom – the sound, which resembles an explosion, that is heard when an aircraft traveling at supersonic speed nears the ground

sound barrier – "wall" that causes a plane to shake, sometimes out of control, when it reaches the speed of sound, which is 660 miles (1,225 kilometers) per hour

streamline – to make an object smoother so it can move more easily through air or water

supersonic – anything that can travel faster than the speed of sound

TIMELINE

February 13: Chuck Yeager born **1923**

U.S. enters World War II **1941** Yeager joins U.S. Air Force

1942 Yeager enters flight-training school

1944

1945 War ends, Yeager becomes test pilot

March: Yeager shot down over France; escapes to Spain

January: Bell X-1 construction completed **1946**

1947

October: Shoots down five enemy planes in one mission

September: Geoffrey de Havilland killed attempting to break the sound barrier **1948** *June:* Air Force announces Yeager's accomplishment

1950 Bell X-1 donated to Smithsonian

November: In a propeller-driven plane, shoots down German jet fighter

May: Yeager begins flight testing Bell X-1

Yeager retires from **1975** U.S. Air Force

October 14: Yeager becomes first human being to break sound barrier

INDEX (*Boldface* page numbers indicate illustrations.)

PHOTO CREDITS

©: Air Forces Flight Test Center History Office: 3, 23, 31 top right; AP/Wide World Photos: 1, 14 bottom, 15, 16, 18, 20, 21, 26, 30 top; Archive Photos: 9, 11, 12, 13, 14 top, 30 bottom; Corbis-Bettmann: 27 right; Superstock, Inc.: 27 left, 29; University of Texas at Dallas, Special Collections: 28 right; UPI/ Corbis-Bettmann: cover, 2, 4, 8, 10, 19, 24, 25, 26 backdrop, 27 backdrop, 28 left, 31 left, 31 bottom right.

Map by TJS Design

ABOUT THE AUTHOR

R. Conrad Stein was born and raised in Chicago, Illinois. He has published more than eighty books for young readers, including many titles in the Cornerstones of Freedom series. Other recent titles Mr. Stein has completed for Children's Press are: *The Assassination of Martin Luther King Jr., The Boston Tea Party, The Battle of the Little Bighorn,* and *The Underground Railroad.*

Mr. Stein currently lives in Chicago with his wife and their daughter, Janna.